North Window

poems by

Emily H. Axelrod

Finishing Line Press
Georgetown, Kentucky

North Window

ACKNOWLEDGMENTS

I have been fortunate to study poetry with gifted teachers. To Katia Kapovich, writer, poet, editor of *Fulcrum, An Annual Anthology of Poetry* and *Aesthetics*, I owe a special debt of gratitude for her unerring instinct, far-ranging knowledge of poetry and literature, and belief in the poet in each of us. Thanks also to Alec Solomita, writer, editor and poet, for his incisive editing, and to Tom Daley, poet and teacher. I also thank my colleagues at Cambridge Center for Adult Education and in the MIT Poetry Group for their thoughtful comments and support over the years.

Publisher: Leah Maines
Editor: Christen Kincaid
Cover Art: Emily H. Axelrod
Author Photo: Clay Oliver
Cover Design: Melissa Winslow Axelrod Design

Order online: www.finishinglinepress.com
            also available on amazon.com

Author inquiries and mail orders:
Finishing Line Press
P. O. Box 1626
Georgetown, Kentucky 40324
U. S. A.

Table of Contents

For Noah and Winnie,
with love unbounded.

I.

Chanel No. 5

I keep your handkerchief
embroidered with blue forget-me-nots,
once fragrant with Chanel No. 5,
and the memory of evenings
I watched you dress,
nights you came to my bedside
to chase away a dream,
or soothe an aching leg.
I hold it against my cheek
in search of a scent long diffused,
suspended in longing and remembrance.

Father

In the photo, my father, tall and lean,
sits on a California lawn, knees bent,
buoyant in fatherhood
and the early days of family.
I am three, hands on his knees,
leaning toward him and laughing.
The black and white image
is glossy with scalloped edges
and faint marks from the photo corners
that once held it in place
in a blue leather album.
Sometimes I forget
those moments,
full of light and promise.

Bureau Drawer

My father's bureau drawer
held treasures.
Atop a stepping stool
I could peer in
and touch the gold locomotive
with moving wheels,
meant for a gentleman's watch chain;
the fountain pen with grandfather's initials,
still spotted with ink, and a tiny orb compass
pointing due north in its dusty habitat.
One day a thief stole them all,
leaving only a broken Timex
with no luster and no history at all.

Dancing Class

When I was invisible
no one asked me to dance.
I watched others on the polished floor
while I stood at the edge,
cloaking my body in shame.
I was impatient for class to end
so I could return to my friend's house
and dissect the evening,
our secret yearnings and our agonies,
safe in the company of girls.

Grandfather Clock

My father wound the grandfather clock
every fifth day. It kept perfect time,
striking each hour, marking day's
passage into night.

When the clock man came
to reassemble the old timepiece
he marveled: zinc weights filled with sand
on cords worn and frayed,
a pendulum of hammered brass,
the moon rising on its face
every day at five.

I do my best to wind the clock,
yet there are weeks it stands silent,
the pendulum still,
time unmeasured,
and the face of the moon
tilts toward evening,
fixed in endless afternoon.

Salt Lake City

In the Nevada desert
we dole out ice cubes
from the dented cooler,
water dripping down our shirts.
Our mothers sing the Mormon hymns
of their childhood in perfect harmony,
and amuse us with stories and riddles.
Heedless of our attention,
they speak in soft voices
of the mysteries of love.

In a treeless parking lot,
we race into the motel pool,
tepid water, deck chairs
faded by desert sun.
How we wish it would never end—
coffee shop dinners with milkshakes,
quarters jingling in slot machines,
tumble of change at a windfall jackpot,
bleached heat, and the chorus of cicadas
in still dry air.

At our grandparents' house
the attic bedroom swelters.
At night our mothers
climb onto the roof
to smoke forbidden cigarettes.
Sunburned and tired,
fighting sleep, we listen,
soothed by their hushed voices
just outside the window.

My Father Says Goodbye

He could not have known,
shuffling ivory dominoes
with practiced hands,
papery skin on bird-like bones.
We played our game,
trading taunts and easy teasing.
After, he checked the locks
and turned the deadbolt,
then climbed the wooden stairs,
fatigued by the effort
of an old and weakened heart.
He paused at the top
to offer a rare embrace
then closed his bedroom door
to sleep.

II.

First Love

We stayed in a cabin
that was once a chicken coop,
facing an open meadow
where our footsteps
bent the damp grass.
On New Year's Eve
we discovered a beach
where towering rock arches
broke the force of waves
on silver-packed sand,
and in the dark chill of evening
we swam the night tide.
I imagine you now
with snapshots of grandchildren
and a row of persimmon trees
where you pluck the ripe fruit,
its flesh still warm
from the California sun.

Tarot

The old mystic lived
in the Redwoods
on a hill above the ocean.
She read my cards one night,
my innocence leaving me helpless
against their dark portent:
Great challenge ahead.
I remembered those cards
in a hospital waiting room
many years later,
knowing they had
foretold the future.

This summer at the fair
amid children with painted faces,
the tarot reader beckoned
and fear rose up like a ghost.
When she turned over
The Charioteer,
Victory over extremes,
I could scarcely listen,
recalling that night
so many years ago.

Hospital Garage

We wind along the spiral ramp
my son and I, among the grey striped
parking spaces where melting snow
leaves black grit and winter dust.
Drivers circle the ramps
carrying balloons to the children
they will visit. For us another appointment,
then a promised visit to the toy store,
where bright lights and rainbow colors
offer a galaxy of choices.

North Window

The window always seemed an intrusion
admitting cold light on fall afternoons,
revealing the neighbors' windows
dotting the rear façade like an advent calendar.
You who crave light on dark winter days
are drawn there, and have made your home
in its north facing glare—drawing board, pencils,
and coffee cups filled with dregs of shortening days
lie scattered on the desktop.
On an afternoon when sun shone through
a leafy scrim during the slow fading of autumn,
it lighted your window and created a tableau
illuminating the arcs and curves
that circumscribe our days.

When My Husband Goes Away

When my husband goes away
I sleep across the bed
with books strewn about me.
I make strong coffee in the morning
and eat an artichoke for dinner.
At night I reach for his pillow
and feel its cool weave on my cheek,
floating in my solitude,
on streams of ideas
through days laced with quiet.

Family Photographs

They seem to picture another family,
babies held gingerly in our arms,
small fingers curled around our own,
birthday parties with plump lips pursed
to blow out four candles.
One by one I take them down,
images muted by afternoon sun
sitting dusty on living room tables,
no longer bright with remembrance.
The flight of years, the yesterdays
stacked one upon another,
buried in the careless annals of memory.

As a Boy

For David

As a boy
you were the one
whose silent tears
fell to the storybook page
when animal heroes
were lost in the forest.

And in the autumn
you could not be consoled
when the furry brown caterpillars
met untimely deaths
beneath our heedless feet.

Each summer
we built ocean tanks
in the backyard
where the starfish, urchin and hermit crab
acted out their lives on a watery stage
as you watched spellbound,
worried by their cannibal ways.

No wonder then that once again
it is the dark spruce
and flowing tide
that offer quiet solace
when life is cruel
and you struggle to understand.

Cosmo

I have a cat who is very old.
When he was young
his fur shone like spun glass;
he climbed trees
and leapt in tall grass,
bringing us field mice
to demonstrate his prowess
and garner our praise.
At home he chased toys the children made,
purposefully stalking paper prey,
jumping into shopping bags they
held open, preening to
their shrieks of delight.

Now he is old
and his fur no longer shines.
We struggle to get him to eat
and give him medicine twice a day.
Mostly he sleeps,
and sometimes he yowls.
He won't climb the apple tree in the spring,
or patrol the edges of the yard
to claim it as his own.
One day soon he will stop eating,
and his drab coat will hang
from protruding bones,
a thick dulled pelt
reminding us of what we have lost.

Museum Café, Paris

Over your shoulder lovers kiss
and children chase a red ball
in and out of the fountain
while their mothers gossip
on a bench nearby.
You speak of the African masks
we have just seen and the paintings,
drenched with color;
I watch romance blossom
and children squabble,
drawn by the sweet allure
of strangers' lives.

Without You

The north windows are papered in rime,
and withered stalks,
some with leaves remaining,
bend against the north wind.
From the kitchen
I listen to windows rattling
and the creaking of weathered boards
in the empty house.
You are far away,
hiking desert trails
among saguaros and tumbleweed,
buoyed by desert sun.

Teacher

The city cascades down hillsides
toward the harbor.
In my room high above the water
I watch a cargo ship,
containers stacked four stories high,
nudged to the dock by two tugs.
Beside the port a Ferris wheel turns
and empty chairs swing in ocean breezes.
I watch, wondering what your day brings
in your classroom across the water.

Red Shoes

I once danced in red shoes
with silver studs and pointed toes,
chic, and a little dangerous.
In those days we sipped dirty martinis
and stayed out until dawn,
careless with time and love.
So many years have melted away
like the Wicked Witch of the West,
but my ruby slippers will dance on.

New Knee

My new knee
won't slow me down
on a wooded path
strewn with roots
and granite shards.
A tidy scar is my badge of courage
or perhaps my scarlet letter
for the sin of pride,
putting my faith in titanium,
believing I might outrun time.

Vows

For Jeff and Melissa

You walk down the aisle on your father's arm,
wrist encircled by a dented bracelet
embossed by budding teeth from
the time your grandmother offered it
to soothe sore gums all those years ago.

You turn to him and speak your vows,
tender and sure and laced with dreams.
We sit close. Our wedding rings
once as sturdy as our promises,
are thin filaments of gold,
circling bent fingers that still recall
the caress of newfound love.

Expecting

For Melissa

I imagine the child in your arms
months from now,
sometimes a daughter
who may prefer mismatched socks
or need red-rimmed glasses
to focus a blurry world,
or perhaps a son
who creates fanciful castles
made of wooden blocks,
and photographs as lyrical
as a summer song.
You will know the tug
of a child at your breast,
eyes seeking yours
with each greedy swallow,
the curl of a small finger
around your own
and a love so tender and consuming
you are forever changed.

Noah Newly Born

For Noah

Your hand curls around my thumb,
heart beating rapidly against my own.
I close my mind to danger,
hurricanes and wars, love and heartbreak,
and imagine myself a bulwark,
fierce protector of your innocence
as I take my first halting steps
beside a life just beginning.

Bath

For Noah

For you my spotted hands
are not marred by time
and my stiffening back
no cause for concern.
As I smooth soap
over your velvet skin,
the curtain of years briefly lifts.
You kick chubby legs
creating small waves,
and oceans of pure delight.

Clock

For Noah

I turn the winder
and weights lift slowly
from the clock's cabinet floor
banging against the old wood
until they are tethered
by the spooled cord.
I nudge the pendulum
to begin its rhythmic tock,
chiming each hour faithfully
as it has for so many years.
You watch from your mother's lap,
transfixed, knowing nothing of time
or the winding down of years.

Information Age

It isn't just the flight of years
or the memories disappearing
silently, without warning,
but the oceans of knowing
approaching like a tsunami,
as thoughts accumulate
faster than our accelerating years,
and the things we took for bedrock
shift into sand, precarious and mutable.

Dandelion

I blow dandelion seeds
into the wind, wishing
with eyes tight shut.
A hundred bracts take flight
on air-light threads,
scattering wishes,
one for the love of a boy
who spun the bottle
and kissed me on a foggy night,
another for the vows
that twined our fates together,
and for the children
we loved with a fervor
that left us breathless.
Now the seeds carry wishes
honed by time, and a few
cling to the flower's head,
out of reach of my softening breath.

Gifts of Age

I am content with freeze or thaw
and trust that the season will turn
despite winds brisk and unrelenting.
I no longer sigh for the softening
of passion and its heartaches,
nor do I rage against our differences,
now a part of my inner landscape
along with questions no longer asked.
Smoke tendrils rise from the chimney
outside the window,
and curl around each other
before thinning into a grey sky.

III.

Bangor Airport

They stand beside the terminal
in desert camouflage
and spotless boots,
names embroidered evenly
across their chests in flawless script,
as if their mothers
had readied them for camp
where they would spend two weeks
sleeping in tents, making new friends,
and singing around the campfire.

Spread out along the walkway
they are a resting flock,
like shore birds standing at ease
in the shallows. From time to time
one or two walk away from the group
with cell phones to their ears,
a mother perhaps, or a lover's goodbye.

Behind the terminal,
the heavy-bellied transport planes,
painted the dark grey of night sky,
wait silently. Soon the young men
will walk into a plane's dark hold,
swallowed like modern Jonahs,
to be lifted from the green spruce
and rocky shores of childhood
to a land of sand and dust
where the enemy hides
in rugged escarpments, waiting.

Mosswood

The old house stands empty,
its showy garden fallow
and brimming with weed.
The broad green door
opens to a window seat
where faded cushions
depict roses and peonies,
forever entwined.
Cracked plates, broken toys
and books bloated with mildew
litter the rooms, debris of past lives.
Upstairs iron bedsteads face the sea
and a pale slant of light
is clouded by dust motes
dancing through stale air.
With each tread the old place sighs,
holding on to the stories
etched in its weathered wood.

Island Girl

Her father built a chicken coop
beneath her bedroom window
where she hears the hens
clucking and cooing all night
under the cold northern sky.
When spring comes
she arrives at our door
with a dozen brown eggs
still warm from the broody hen
who squawked and flapped
when she reached beneath its ruffled breast
to gather the eggs,
sweet with the smell of straw.

Flotilla

for Hugh

The line of boats
curves around the point
heading into the cove
where he played as a boy
in tide pools alive with periwinkle and crab.
The shore dips to a deep bowl
tumbling rocks to a smooth sheen
while boats drift together.
We listen to the minister
entrust him to his god.
Flower petals float on the surface,
marking the place
where he is returned to the sea
that claimed him so unexpectedly,
on a spring morning filled with promise.

Winter Sea

I bend into the wind
against frigid salt spray.
The ocean breaks dark grey
along the empty strand
and on the far horizon
fishing boats are tossed like confetti.
Beneath my feet a fisherman's glove,
edged in rime, protrudes from the ice;
rounded granite stones
and shards of mussel shell
cluster in a frozen tableau, winter's ephemera,
elegant recital for the practiced eye.

For C.C.

You were found on a bed of moss
in your sanctuary in the woods,
lifted by birdsong
to your own personal god.
On that day, unaware,
I bought a new red lipstick
the color of cinnabar,
and walked under fall leaves
brilliant with death.

IV.

After Christmas

Spruce needles scatter to the floor
in a fragrant blizzard
as I lift ornaments from the tree,
wrapping them in brittle tissue
unfolded weeks before.
Carved sleds with the children's names,
a straw star that tilts atop the tree,
and a balsa ark with animals two by two.
I tug the tree to the sidewalk
where it lies in formation
with neighbors' castoffs,
lifeless remains of holiday cheer.

Frozen bits of confetti
lie entombed, paper stars
in a motionless firmament,
and in storefronts in town,
Mary and Joseph kneel
by bags of ice melt and sand.
Today the sun will set at 4:29
And most of our waking
will be in darkness.
By next week 4:36
as we begin the slow march
toward the light.

February

The spoon from the drawer
is cold to the touch
and draws heat from
the steaming cup.

A neighbor hangs
from her window
swiping at icicles
with a broomstick
and grim resolve.

White light
polishes the air
as a shard of ice snaps
and falls to the ground.

Drought

Skies darken in late afternoon
with rain that will not fall,
an occasional crack of lightning
a fiery exclamation point.
On the ground streams dwindle,
coating rocks with murky algae
that blooms in the meager flow.
Well water tastes of minerals and mud;
we ration it like misers.
Only the Valley Oaks seemed unperturbed,
bending their sculpted trunks
to the brown grass,
and taking root once more,
tentacles burrowing into desiccated soil,
leaves shiny and sharp.

Wildfire

Brown grasses that once bent
against the coming breeze,
their tawny stalks swaying in fluid waves,
are now dark embers.
Mesquite and Manzanita whose smooth red stems
are the sculpture of the grassland,
burned like tinder,
and the smoldering oaks
that bent to the ground were easy prey
for flames that leapt their gnarled trunks
leaving them charred and smoking.
On a winter day the rains will come
and in spring green shoots will appear,
brilliant against the charcoal remains.

Derby

On Derby day the air is thick
and horses' coats shine
as they arch their necks,
lifting slender legs
of muscle taut and honed.
The jockeys' silks glow
as they perch high on their horses' haunches,
whispering to them in a lover's voice,
urgent and filled with promise.
At the start the horses leap in a single motion,
all stride, all extension.
Then one takes flight,
floating above the muddy turf,
the jockey clinging to his lathered neck
as they circle the track
passing the finish in a sprint,
barely slowing, ready to run forever.

Art Studio

The skeleton hangs askew
from a metal stand, head bowed.
Its single arm dangles,
radius and ulna in parallel arcs,
joined neatly at the wrist.
The curving ribcage,
the elegant beauty of bones
that once encircled a living heart
lifts in perfect symmetry.
An artist's hand, long fingers
that could have played Bach,
reaching across octaves for the high notes.
On the bony face, jaws are filled
with a perfect array of teeth,
the semblance of a smile.
What clues lie within my bones,
still wrapped in muscle and sinew,
attuned to the rhythm of a beating heart.

Three Houses

My neighbor studies the stars
and grows tomatoes,
plump and warm
from the summer sun.
I plant flowers in my backyard
pulling weeds from black soil
that was once a stream bed.
In the house between,
the plants are never trimmed,
and engulf the path to the door.
The front stairs are rotting
from the damp shade;
not even the postman
dares set foot upon them.

Widow

I no longer hear their quarrels
or meet him mumbling angrily to himself
as he walks their grizzled dog.
Does she mourn for him
and the loss of their bellicose love,
or is she settling comfortably
into the long silence?
When I meet her on the sidewalk
she speaks with her gaze
far from where we stand.
Is she seeing ghosts
or just the leaves turning to crimson
on the old maple up the street?

The Comcast Man

The Comcast Man came right on time,
thin and sullen, then paused
to place paper booties on his shoes
to protect the aging carpet.
He spoke softly with a heavy accent
skimming fingers across the keyboard
as he coaxed secrets to the screen.
He remarked the frayed wires
hanging loosely outside the window,
then disappeared into his truck,
a shiny coil soon installed.
I wondered what odyssey
brought this man to my doorstep,
quiet and knowing, and full of secrets.

Winter Morning

A plough blade
scrapes the frozen pavement,
raising sparks
as it scours the asphalt,
back and forth
until the surface gleams
black and cold.
You lie in a hospital bed
lulled by the slow drip
of the IV bag, no longer distinct
through deaf ears.
The books you have written
are stacked near the bed
as if to remind you
of work still to be done.
In the waiting room
a piece of sky is framed
by one anonymous window.
Outside snow continues to fall.

Yellow House

The house where the old woman
Once bathed in autumn sun,
bundled against the oncoming cold
on a lopsided rickety chaise,
now gleams with fresh yellow paint.
The cracked and dirty windows
where a peace sign yellowed
and curled with age, have been replaced
with new ones, their labels facing the street.
The twisted brown grass in the weedy garden
will soon be replaced by shapely evergreens
and politely blooming roses,
thoroughly mulched and symmetrically arranged,
erasing any trace of the woman
who rested in her wild and overgrown garden.

Mourners Kaddish

The temple is full of strangers
or, more accurately
the room is full of people
who know each other,
and I am a stranger.
Eulogies are vivid;
I begin to think I know him,
but it isn't true.
I only know the sadness
in the eyes of his sons,
and that medicines bought time,
and more time, until time ran out.
I sit in the warmth of the congregation,
a wanderer in the world of the devout
wondering at the meaning
of so terrible a loss.
Awash in doubt,
I recite the Mourner's Kaddish.

V.

In the Marais

The old woman dances
to the tunes of the jazz band,
following them from corner to corner
around the Marais.
Her fitted wool coat
the color of deep forest,
a matching cap atop grey hair.
When the saxophone sounds
its first bluesy notes,
the trombone joins
and she begins to move,
holding her coat away from her hips
in wrinkled hands,
swaying to the music
with a coquettish smile.
I can see the girl
dancing with her lover
on a moonlit night on the Seine.

Istanbul

In Istanbul the call to prayer
rouses us from sleep.
Siren song of the devout,
the voice of the muezzuin
echoes through ancient streets.

In the Blue Mosque
painted tiles depict flower,
fruit and cypress.
Light the color of lapis
filters the winter sun,
and casts a pall on our
pale complexions.

Men face east and bend
to kiss the floor.
I turn away from the intimacy
of their devotion.

Tailloire

We travelled to a place
where jagged mountains
rise from a turquoise lake
and weathered houses
shaded by fruit trees
spill down to the shore.
Each day in late afternoon,
we floated on crystalline water,
as light a flotsam
weightless and in awe.

Night Flight

For twenty days we traveled
in our small band,
climbing ancient amphitheaters
built of stones as tall as a man.

We gaped at eerie forms
on a valley floor
where volcanic ash
spread like baker's flour
to be shaped and kneaded
by swirling desert winds.

On the plane ride home
we flew over oceans
and traveled across time
falling slowly into ourselves,
searching for the lives we left behind.

Emily H. Axelrod's poems are concerned with family, fleeting moments embedded in memory, the mysteries of the natural world, and with the joys and struggles of daily life. Her poems draw upon a childhood in San Francisco, her abiding love for Northern California, family, and travel. She lives in Cambridge, MA and spends summers on a small island in Maine. Her husband, two adult children and two grandchildren appear throughout the book.

Ms. Axelrod's professional background was in the world of architecture and urban planning, where she worked both in public agencies and private firms in San Francisco and Boston. She is a graduate of the Harvard Graduate School of Design, and the former Director of the Rudy Bruner Award for Urban Excellence, a national award for urban places. Her career in the design profession informs her poetry in many ways, particularly in its strong visual orientation.